Review
Multiplication 1

To parents

Your child will first review multiplication from one to five. If your child encounters difficulty during this review, perhaps some extended review with *My Book of Simple Multiplication* would be a good idea.

■ Multiply the numbers below.

(1) 1 × 1 =

(2) 1 × 2 =

(3) 1 × 3 =

(4) 1 × 4 =

(5) 1 × 5 =

(6) 1 × 6 =

(7) 1 × 7 =

(8) 1 × 8 =

(9) 1 × 9 =

(10) 1 × 10 =

(11) 1 × 7 =

(12) 1 × 8 =

(13) 1 × 10 =

(14) 1 × 9 =

(15) 1 × 2 =

(16) 1 × 6 =

(17) 1 × 5 =

(18) 1 × 4 =

(19) 1 × 3 =

(20) 1 × 1 =

Multiplication I

■ Multiply the numbers below.

(1) $1 \times 9 =$

(2) $1 \times 7 =$

(3) $1 \times 5 =$

(4) $1 \times 1 =$

(5) $1 \times 4 =$

(6) $1 \times 8 =$

(7) $1 \times 6 =$

(8) $1 \times 3 =$

(9) $1 \times 10 =$

(10) $1 \times 2 =$

(11) $1 \times 1 =$

(12) $1 \times 10 =$

(13) $1 \times 3 =$

(14) $1 \times 7 =$

(15) $1 \times 9 =$

(16) $1 \times 6 =$

(17) $1 \times 2 =$

(18) $1 \times 4 =$

(19) $1 \times 8 =$

(20) $1 \times 5 =$

Name

Date

■ Multiply the numbers below.

(1) $2 \times 1 =$

(2) $2 \times 2 =$

(3) $2 \times 3 =$

(4) $2 \times 4 =$

(5) $2 \times 5 =$

(6) $2 \times 6 =$

(7) $2 \times 7 =$

(8) $2 \times 8 =$

(9) $2 \times 9 =$

(10) $2 \times 10 =$

(11) $2 \times 3 =$

(12) $2 \times 8 =$

(13) $2 \times 9 =$

(14) $2 \times 10 =$

(15) $2 \times 2 =$

(16) $2 \times 4 =$

(17) $2 \times 6 =$

(18) $2 \times 7 =$

(19) $2 \times 5 =$

(20) $2 \times 1 =$

Multiplication 2

■ Multiply the numbers below.

(1) $2 \times 2 =$

(2) $2 \times 4 =$

(3) $2 \times 8 =$

(4) $2 \times 10 =$

(5) $2 \times 1 =$

(6) $2 \times 3 =$

(7) $2 \times 5 =$

(8) $2 \times 7 =$

(9) $2 \times 9 =$

(10) $2 \times 6 =$

(11) $2 \times 7 =$

(12) $2 \times 2 =$

(13) $2 \times 5 =$

(14) $2 \times 9 =$

(15) $2 \times 3 =$

(16) $2 \times 10 =$

(17) $2 \times 4 =$

(18) $2 \times 1 =$

(19) $2 \times 6 =$

(20) $2 \times 8 =$

Review
Multiplication 3

■ Multiply the numbers below.

(1) $3 \times 1 =$

(2) $3 \times 2 =$

(3) $3 \times 3 =$

(4) $3 \times 4 =$

(5) $3 \times 5 =$

(6) $3 \times 6 =$

(7) $3 \times 7 =$

(8) $3 \times 8 =$

(9) $3 \times 9 =$

(10) $3 \times 10 =$

(11) $3 \times 2 =$

(12) $3 \times 3 =$

(13) $3 \times 10 =$

(14) $3 \times 4 =$

(15) $3 \times 1 =$

(16) $3 \times 5 =$

(17) $3 \times 6 =$

(18) $3 \times 8 =$

(19) $3 \times 9 =$

(20) $3 \times 7 =$

Multiplication 3

■ Multiply the numbers below.

(1) $3 \times 3 =$

(11) $3 \times 5 =$

(2) $3 \times 7 =$

(12) $3 \times 8 =$

(3) $3 \times 9 =$

(13) $3 \times 6 =$

(4) $3 \times 1 =$

(14) $3 \times 10 =$

(5) $3 \times 2 =$

(15) $3 \times 2 =$

(6) $3 \times 10 =$

(16) $3 \times 4 =$

(7) $3 \times 6 =$

(17) $3 \times 1 =$

(8) $3 \times 4 =$

(18) $3 \times 7 =$

(9) $3 \times 5 =$

(19) $3 \times 9 =$

(10) $3 \times 8 =$

(20) $3 \times 3 =$

4 Review
Multiplication 4

Name

Date

■ Multiply the numbers below.

(1) $4 \times 1 =$

(2) $4 \times 2 =$

(3) $4 \times 3 =$

(4) $4 \times 4 =$

(5) $4 \times 5 =$

(6) $4 \times 6 =$

(7) $4 \times 7 =$

(8) $4 \times 8 =$

(9) $4 \times 9 =$

(10) $4 \times 10 =$

(11) $4 \times 3 =$

(12) $4 \times 6 =$

(13) $4 \times 9 =$

(14) $4 \times 5 =$

(15) $4 \times 1 =$

(16) $4 \times 10 =$

(17) $4 \times 8 =$

(18) $4 \times 7 =$

(19) $4 \times 2 =$

(20) $4 \times 4 =$

Multiplication 4

■ Multiply the numbers below.

(1) $4 \times 6 =$

(2) $4 \times 4 =$

(3) $4 \times 10 =$

(4) $4 \times 3 =$

(5) $4 \times 5 =$

(6) $4 \times 1 =$

(7) $4 \times 2 =$

(8) $4 \times 7 =$

(9) $4 \times 9 =$

(10) $4 \times 8 =$

(11) $4 \times 7 =$

(12) $4 \times 8 =$

(13) $4 \times 1 =$

(14) $4 \times 9 =$

(15) $4 \times 5 =$

(16) $4 \times 10 =$

(17) $4 \times 4 =$

(18) $4 \times 6 =$

(19) $4 \times 2 =$

(20) $4 \times 3 =$

Review
Multiplication 5

■ Multiply the numbers below.

(1) $5 \times 1 =$

(2) $5 \times 2 =$

(3) $5 \times 3 =$

(4) $5 \times 4 =$

(5) $5 \times 5 =$

(6) $5 \times 6 =$

(7) $5 \times 7 =$

(8) $5 \times 8 =$

(9) $5 \times 9 =$

(10) $5 \times 10 =$

(11) $5 \times 2 =$

(12) $5 \times 4 =$

(13) $5 \times 8 =$

(14) $5 \times 1 =$

(15) $5 \times 10 =$

(16) $5 \times 9 =$

(17) $5 \times 7 =$

(18) $5 \times 6 =$

(19) $5 \times 3 =$

(20) $5 \times 5 =$

Multiplication 5

■ Multiply the numbers below.

(1) $5 \times 3 =$

(2) $5 \times 5 =$

(3) $5 \times 7 =$

(4) $5 \times 4 =$

(5) $5 \times 10 =$

(6) $5 \times 1 =$

(7) $5 \times 2 =$

(8) $5 \times 9 =$

(9) $5 \times 6 =$

(10) $5 \times 8 =$

(11) $5 \times 6 =$

(12) $5 \times 10 =$

(13) $5 \times 3 =$

(14) $5 \times 7 =$

(15) $5 \times 1 =$

(16) $5 \times 4 =$

(17) $5 \times 9 =$

(18) $5 \times 2 =$

(19) $5 \times 8 =$

(20) $5 \times 5 =$

Review

Multiplication 1–5

■ Multiply the numbers below.

(1) $1 \times 3 =$

(2) $2 \times 4 =$

(3) $3 \times 5 =$

(4) $4 \times 6 =$

(5) $5 \times 7 =$

(6) $1 \times 6 =$

(7) $2 \times 7 =$

(8) $3 \times 8 =$

(9) $4 \times 9 =$

(10) $5 \times 10 =$

(11) $1 \times 7 =$

(12) $2 \times 9 =$

(13) $3 \times 2 =$

(14) $4 \times 3 =$

(15) $5 \times 2 =$

(16) $1 \times 2 =$

(17) $2 \times 6 =$

(18) $3 \times 7 =$

(19) $4 \times 5 =$

(20) $5 \times 9 =$

Multiplication 1-5

■ Multiply the numbers below.

(1) $1 \times 9 =$

(2) $2 \times 4 =$

(3) $3 \times 6 =$

(4) $4 \times 8 =$

(5) $5 \times 3 =$

(6) $1 \times 6 =$

(7) $2 \times 7 =$

(8) $3 \times 3 =$

(9) $4 \times 5 =$

(10) $5 \times 2 =$

(11) $1 \times 3 =$

(12) $4 \times 6 =$

(13) $3 \times 8 =$

(14) $2 \times 9 =$

(15) $4 \times 1 =$

(16) $5 \times 4 =$

(17) $2 \times 6 =$

(18) $3 \times 7 =$

(19) $1 \times 4 =$

(20) $5 \times 10 =$

7 Practicing Numbers
1 – 60

Name

Date

To parents
Skip counting and repeated addition are good ways to prepare for multiplication. In order to help your child see the link between multiplication and skip counting, point out that they are tracing the multiples of six in the charts below, for example.

■ Say each number aloud as you trace it.

1	2	3	4	5	6	7	8	9	10
11	12	13	14	15	16	17	18	19	20
21	22	23	24	25	26	27	28	29	30
31	32	33	34	35	36	37	38	39	40
41	42	43	44	45	46	47	48	49	50
51	52	53	54	55	56	57	58	59	60
61	62	63	64	65	66	67	68	69	70
71	72	73	74	75	76	77	78	79	80
81	82	83	84	85	86	87	88	89	90
91	92	93	94	95	96	97	98	99	100

6	12	18	24	30	36	42	48	54	60

■ Draw a line from 6 to 60 in order while saying each number aloud.

■ Add the numbers below.

(1)　6 + 6 = 12

(2)　6 + 6 + 6 = 18

(3)　6 + 6 + 6 + 6 = 24

(4)　6 + 6 + 6 + 6 + 6 = 30

(5)　6 + 6 + 6 + 6 + 6 + 6 = 36

(6)　6 + 6 + 6 + 6 + 6 + 6 + 6 = 42

(7)　6 + 6 + 6 + 6 + 6 + 6 + 6 + 6 = 48

(8)　6 + 6 + 6 + 6 + 6 + 6 + 6 + 6 + 6 = 54

(9)　6 + 6 + 6 + 6 + 6 + 6 + 6 + 6 + 6 + 6 = 60

8 Practicing Repeated Addition

6-30

Name

Date

To parents
Repeated addition is good preparation for multiplication. In order to help your child see the link between multiplication and repeated addition, ask him or her how many sixes there are in the number sentences below, for example.

■ Say each number aloud as you trace it.

6	12	18	24	30

(1) $6 + 6 = 12$

(2) $6 + 6 + 6 = 18$

(3) $6 + 6 + 6 + 6 = 24$

(4) $6 + 6 + 6 + 6 + 6 = 30$

■ Write the numbers on the number line. Then add the numbers below.

6				

(1) $6 + 6 =$

(2) $6 + 6 + 6 =$

(3) $6 + 6 + 6 + 6 =$

(4) $6 + 6 + 6 + 6 + 6 =$

■ Say each number aloud as you trace it.

| 36 | 42 | 48 | 54 | 60 |

(1) $6+6+6+6+6+6 = 36$

(2) $6+6+6+6+6+6+6 = 42$

(3) $6+6+6+6+6+6+6+6 = 48$

(4) $6+6+6+6+6+6+6+6+6 = 54$

(5) $6+6+6+6+6+6+6+6+6+6 = 60$

■ Write the numbers in the number line. Then add the numbers below.

| 36 | | | |

(1) $6+6+6+6+6+6 =$

(2) $6+6+6+6+6+6+6 =$

(3) $6+6+6+6+6+6+6+6 =$

(4) $6+6+6+6+6+6+6+6+6 =$

(5) $6+6+6+6+6+6+6+6+6+6 =$

9 Multiplication 6

6×1 to 6×10

Name

Date

To parents

From this page on, your child will practice the multiplication tables for the number 6 through 10. If your child has difficulty understanding these number sentences, help him or her understand that 6 × 3 is "three groups of six," for example.

■ Read the multiplication table aloud.

Multiplication Table

(1) 6 × 1 = 6   Six times one is six.

(2) 6 × 2 = 12   Six times two is twelve.

(3) 6 × 3 = 18   Six times three is eighteen.

(4) 6 × 4 = 24   Six times four is twenty-four.

(5) 6 × 5 = 30   Six times five is thirty.

(6) 6 × 6 = 36   Six times six is thirty-six.

(7) 6 × 7 = 42   Six times seven is forty-two.

(8) 6 × 8 = 48   Six times eight is forty-eight.

(9) 6 × 9 = 54   Six times nine is fifty-four.

(10) 6 × 10 = 60   Six times ten is sixty.

■ Read each number sentence aloud as you trace the answer.

(1) 6 × 1 = 6

(2) 6 × 2 = 12

(3) 6 × 3 = 18

(4) 6 × 4 = 24

(5) 6 × 5 = 30

(6) 6 × 6 = 36

(7) 6 × 7 = 42

(8) 6 × 8 = 48

(9) 6 × 9 = 54

(10) 6 × 10 = 60

6×1 to 6×10

■ Multiply the numbers below.

(1) 6 × 1 =

(2) 6 × 2 =

(3) 6 × 3 =

(4) 6 × 4 =

(5) 6 × 5 =

(6) 6 × 6 =

(7) 6 × 7 =

(8) 6 × 8 =

(9) 6 × 9 =

(10) 6 × 10 =

(11) 6 × 1 =

(12) 6 × 2 =

(13) 6 × 3 =

(14) 6 × 4 =

(15) 6 × 5 =

(16) 6 × 6 =

(17) 6 × 7 =

(18) 6 × 8 =

(19) 6 × 9 =

(20) 6 × 10 =

10 Multiplication 6
6×1 to 6×10

Name

Date

■ Multiply the numbers below.

(1) $6 \times 3 =$

(2) $6 \times 6 =$

(3) $6 \times 9 =$

(4) $6 \times 5 =$

(5) $6 \times 1 =$

(6) $6 \times 7 =$

(7) $6 \times 2 =$

(8) $6 \times 8 =$

(9) $6 \times 10 =$

(10) $6 \times 4 =$

(11) $6 \times 9 =$

(12) $6 \times 1 =$

(13) $6 \times 7 =$

(14) $6 \times 10 =$

(15) $6 \times 8 =$

(16) $6 \times 3 =$

(17) $6 \times 5 =$

(18) $6 \times 2 =$

(19) $6 \times 4 =$

(20) $6 \times 6 =$

■ Multiply the numbers below.

(1) $6 \times 4 =$

(2) $6 \times 7 =$

(3) $6 \times 10 =$

(4) $6 \times 2 =$

(5) $6 \times 6 =$

(6) $6 \times 1 =$

(7) $6 \times 8 =$

(8) $6 \times 3 =$

(9) $6 \times 9 =$

(10) $6 \times 5 =$

(11) $6 \times 9 =$

(12) $6 \times 3 =$

(13) $6 \times 1 =$

(14) $6 \times 4 =$

(15) $6 \times 10 =$

(16) $6 \times 5 =$

(17) $6 \times 7 =$

(18) $6 \times 2 =$

(19) $6 \times 8 =$

(20) $6 \times 6 =$

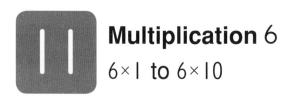

Multiplication 6

6×1 to 6×10

Name

Date

■ Multiply the numbers below.

(1) 6 × 7 =

(2) 6 × 3 =

(3) 6 × 6 =

(4) 6 × 1 =

(5) 6 × 10 =

(6) 6 × 5 =

(7) 6 × 9 =

(8) 6 × 4 =

(9) 6 × 2 =

(10) 6 × 8 =

(11) 6 × 2 =

(12) 6 × 5 =

(13) 6 × 9 =

(14) 6 × 7 =

(15) 6 × 3 =

(16) 6 × 1 =

(17) 6 × 8 =

(18) 6 × 6 =

(19) 6 × 4 =

(20) 6 × 10 =

■ Multiply the numbers below.

(1) $6 \times 1 =$

(2) $6 \times 8 =$

(3) $6 \times 10 =$

(4) $6 \times 3 =$

(5) $6 \times 6 =$

(6) $6 \times 2 =$

(7) $6 \times 7 =$

(8) $6 \times 4 =$

(9) $6 \times 5 =$

(10) $6 \times 9 =$

(11) $6 \times 4 =$

(12) $6 \times 9 =$

(13) $6 \times 1 =$

(14) $6 \times 5 =$

(15) $6 \times 10 =$

(16) $6 \times 6 =$

(17) $6 \times 2 =$

(18) $6 \times 8 =$

(19) $6 \times 3 =$

(20) $6 \times 7 =$

Practicing Numbers
1–70

Name

Date

■ Say each number aloud as you trace it.

1	2	3	4	5	6	7	8	9	10
11	12	13	14	15	16	17	18	19	20
21	22	23	24	25	26	27	28	29	30
31	32	33	34	35	36	37	38	39	40
41	42	43	44	45	46	47	48	49	50
51	52	53	54	55	56	57	58	59	60
61	62	63	64	65	66	67	68	69	70
71	72	73	74	75	76	77	78	79	80
81	82	83	84	85	86	87	88	89	90
91	92	93	94	95	96	97	98	99	100

7	14	21	28	35	42	49	56	63	70

■ Draw a line from 7 to 70 in order while saying each number aloud.

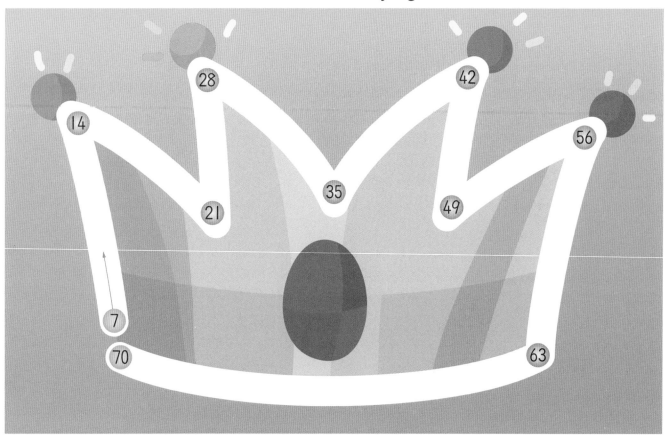

■ Add the numbers below.

(1) $7 + 7 = 14$

(2) $7 + 7 + 7 = 21$

(3) $7 + 7 + 7 + 7 = 28$

(4) $7 + 7 + 7 + 7 + 7 = 35$

(5) $7 + 7 + 7 + 7 + 7 + 7 = 42$

(6) $7 + 7 + 7 + 7 + 7 + 7 + 7 = 49$

(7) $7 + 7 + 7 + 7 + 7 + 7 + 7 + 7 = 56$

(8) $7 + 7 + 7 + 7 + 7 + 7 + 7 + 7 + 7 = 63$

(9) $7 + 7 + 7 + 7 + 7 + 7 + 7 + 7 + 7 + 7 = 70$

13 Practicing Repeated Addition

7–35

To parents

Repeated addition is good preparation for multiplication. In order to help your child see the link between multiplication and repeated addition, ask him or her how many sevens there are in the number sentences below, for example.

Name

Date

■ Say each number aloud as you trace it.

| 7 | 14 | 21 | 28 | 35 |

(1) $7 + 7 = 14$

(2) $7 + 7 + 7 = 21$

(3) $7 + 7 + 7 + 7 = 28$

(4) $7 + 7 + 7 + 7 + 7 = 35$

■ Write the numbers on the number line. Then add the numbers below.

| 7 | | | | |

(1) $7 + 7 =$

(2) $7 + 7 + 7 =$

(3) $7 + 7 + 7 + 7 =$

(4) $7 + 7 + 7 + 7 + 7 =$

■ Say each number aloud as you trace it.

| 42 | 49 | 56 | 63 | 70 |

(1) 7 + 7 + 7 + 7 + 7 + 7 = 42

(2) 7 + 7 + 7 + 7 + 7 + 7 + 7 = 49

(3) 7 + 7 + 7 + 7 + 7 + 7 + 7 + 7 = 56

(4) 7 + 7 + 7 + 7 + 7 + 7 + 7 + 7 + 7 = 63

(5) 7 + 7 + 7 + 7 + 7 + 7 + 7 + 7 + 7 + 7 = 70

■ Write the numbers in the number line. Then add the numbers below.

| 42 | | | |

(1) 7 + 7 + 7 + 7 + 7 + 7 =

(2) 7 + 7 + 7 + 7 + 7 + 7 + 7 =

(3) 7 + 7 + 7 + 7 + 7 + 7 + 7 + 7 =

(4) 7 + 7 + 7 + 7 + 7 + 7 + 7 + 7 + 7 =

(5) 7 + 7 + 7 + 7 + 7 + 7 + 7 + 7 + 7 + 7 =

Name	
Date	

■ Read the multiplication table aloud.

Multiplication Table

(1) $7 \times 1 = 7$ Seven times one is seven.

(2) $7 \times 2 = 14$ Seven times two is fourteen.

(3) $7 \times 3 = 21$ Seven times three is twenty-one.

(4) $7 \times 4 = 28$ Seven times four is twenty-eight.

(5) $7 \times 5 = 35$ Seven times five is thirty-five.

(6) $7 \times 6 = 42$ Seven times six is forty-two.

(7) $7 \times 7 = 49$ Seven times seven is forty-nine.

(8) $7 \times 8 = 56$ Seven times eight is fifty-six.

(9) $7 \times 9 = 63$ Seven times nine is sixty-three.

(10) $7 \times 10 = 70$ Seven times ten is seventy.

■ Read each number sentence aloud as you trace the answer.

(1) $7 \times 1 = 7$ (6) $7 \times 6 = 42$

(2) $7 \times 2 = 14$ (7) $7 \times 7 = 49$

(3) $7 \times 3 = 21$ (8) $7 \times 8 = 56$

(4) $7 \times 4 = 28$ (9) $7 \times 9 = 63$

(5) $7 \times 5 = 35$ (10) $7 \times 10 = 70$

■ Multiply the numbers below.

(1) $7 \times 1 =$

(2) $7 \times 2 =$

(3) $7 \times 3 =$

(4) $7 \times 4 =$

(5) $7 \times 5 =$

(6) $7 \times 6 =$

(7) $7 \times 7 =$

(8) $7 \times 8 =$

(9) $7 \times 9 =$

(10) $7 \times 10 =$

(11) $7 \times 1 =$

(12) $7 \times 2 =$

(13) $7 \times 3 =$

(14) $7 \times 4 =$

(15) $7 \times 5 =$

(16) $7 \times 6 =$

(17) $7 \times 7 =$

(18) $7 \times 8 =$

(19) $7 \times 9 =$

(20) $7 \times 10 =$

Multiplication 7

7×1 to 7×10

Name

Date

■ Multiply the numbers below.

(1) $7 \times 3 =$

(2) $7 \times 6 =$

(3) $7 \times 9 =$

(4) $7 \times 5 =$

(5) $7 \times 1 =$

(6) $7 \times 7 =$

(7) $7 \times 2 =$

(8) $7 \times 8 =$

(9) $7 \times 10 =$

(10) $7 \times 4 =$

(11) $7 \times 9 =$

(12) $7 \times 1 =$

(13) $7 \times 7 =$

(14) $7 \times 10 =$

(15) $7 \times 8 =$

(16) $7 \times 3 =$

(17) $7 \times 5 =$

(18) $7 \times 2 =$

(19) $7 \times 4 =$

(20) $7 \times 6 =$

■ **Multiply the numbers below.**

(1) $7 \times 4 =$

(2) $7 \times 7 =$

(3) $7 \times 10 =$

(4) $7 \times 2 =$

(5) $7 \times 6 =$

(6) $7 \times 1 =$

(7) $7 \times 8 =$

(8) $7 \times 3 =$

(9) $7 \times 9 =$

(10) $7 \times 5 =$

(11) $7 \times 9 =$

(12) $7 \times 3 =$

(13) $7 \times 1 =$

(14) $7 \times 4 =$

(15) $7 \times 10 =$

(16) $7 \times 5 =$

(17) $7 \times 7 =$

(18) $7 \times 2 =$

(19) $7 \times 8 =$

(20) $7 \times 6 =$

16 Multiplication 7
7×1 to 7×10

Name

Date

■ Multiply the numbers below.

(1) $7 \times 7 =$

(2) $7 \times 3 =$

(3) $7 \times 6 =$

(4) $7 \times 1 =$

(5) $7 \times 10 =$

(6) $7 \times 5 =$

(7) $7 \times 9 =$

(8) $7 \times 4 =$

(9) $7 \times 2 =$

(10) $7 \times 8 =$

(11) $7 \times 2 =$

(12) $7 \times 5 =$

(13) $7 \times 9 =$

(14) $7 \times 7 =$

(15) $7 \times 3 =$

(16) $7 \times 1 =$

(17) $7 \times 8 =$

(18) $7 \times 6 =$

(19) $7 \times 4 =$

(20) $7 \times 10 =$

7×1 to 7×10

■ Multiply the numbers below.

(1) 7 × 1 =

(2) 7 × 8 =

(3) 7 × 10 =

(4) 7 × 3 =

(5) 7 × 6 =

(6) 7 × 2 =

(7) 7 × 7 =

(8) 7 × 4 =

(9) 7 × 5 =

(10) 7 × 9 =

(11) 7 × 4 =

(12) 7 × 9 =

(13) 7 × 1 =

(14) 7 × 5 =

(15) 7 × 10 =

(16) 7 × 6 =

(17) 7 × 2 =

(18) 7 × 8 =

(19) 7 × 3 =

(20) 7 × 7 =

Review

Multiplication 6, 7

■ Multiply the numbers below.

(1) $6 \times 1 =$

(2) $6 \times 2 =$

(3) $6 \times 3 =$

(4) $6 \times 4 =$

(5) $6 \times 5 =$

(6) $6 \times 6 =$

(7) $6 \times 7 =$

(8) $6 \times 8 =$

(9) $6 \times 9 =$

(10) $6 \times 10 =$

(11) $7 \times 1 =$

(12) $7 \times 2 =$

(13) $7 \times 3 =$

(14) $7 \times 4 =$

(15) $7 \times 5 =$

(16) $7 \times 6 =$

(17) $7 \times 7 =$

(18) $7 \times 8 =$

(19) $7 \times 9 =$

(20) $7 \times 10 =$

Multiplication 6, 7

■ Multiply the numbers below.

(1) $7 \times 9 =$

(2) $6 \times 7 =$

(3) $7 \times 5 =$

(4) $6 \times 6 =$

(5) $7 \times 1 =$

(6) $6 \times 8 =$

(7) $7 \times 10 =$

(8) $6 \times 3 =$

(9) $7 \times 2 =$

(10) $6 \times 4 =$

(11) $6 \times 10 =$

(12) $7 \times 3 =$

(13) $6 \times 1 =$

(14) $7 \times 8 =$

(15) $6 \times 5 =$

(16) $7 \times 6 =$

(17) $6 \times 2 =$

(18) $7 \times 4 =$

(19) $6 \times 9 =$

(20) $7 \times 7 =$

Name

Date

■ Say each number aloud as you trace it.

1	2	3	4	5	6	7	8	9	10
11	12	13	14	15	16	17	18	19	20
21	22	23	24	25	26	27	28	29	30
31	32	33	34	35	36	37	38	39	40
41	42	43	44	45	46	47	48	49	50
51	52	53	54	55	56	57	58	59	60
61	62	63	64	65	66	67	68	69	70
71	72	73	74	75	76	77	78	79	80
81	82	83	84	85	86	87	88	89	90
91	92	93	94	95	96	97	98	99	100

8	16	24	32	40	48	56	64	72	80

■ Draw a line from 8 to 80 in order while saying each number aloud.

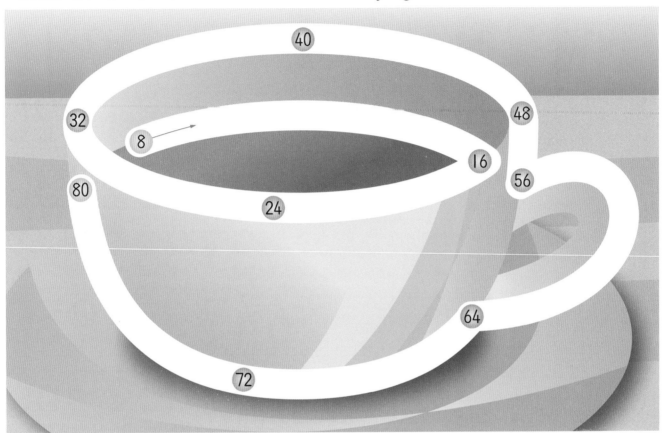

■ Add the numbers below.

(1) $8 + 8 = 16$

(2) $8 + 8 + 8 = 24$

(3) $8 + 8 + 8 + 8 = 32$

(4) $8 + 8 + 8 + 8 + 8 = 40$

(5) $8 + 8 + 8 + 8 + 8 + 8 = 48$

(6) $8 + 8 + 8 + 8 + 8 + 8 + 8 = 56$

(7) $8 + 8 + 8 + 8 + 8 + 8 + 8 + 8 = 64$

(8) $8 + 8 + 8 + 8 + 8 + 8 + 8 + 8 + 8 = 72$

(9) $8 + 8 + 8 + 8 + 8 + 8 + 8 + 8 + 8 + 8 = 80$

Name

Date

■ Say each number aloud as you trace it.

8	16	24	32	40

(1) $8 + 8 = 16$

(2) $8 + 8 + 8 = 24$

(3) $8 + 8 + 8 + 8 = 32$

(4) $8 + 8 + 8 + 8 + 8 = 40$

■ Write the numbers on the number line. Then add the numbers below.

8				

(1) $8 + 8 =$

(2) $8 + 8 + 8 =$

(3) $8 + 8 + 8 + 8 =$

(4) $8 + 8 + 8 + 8 + 8 =$

■ Say each number aloud as you trace it.

| 48 | 56 | 64 | 72 | 80 |

(1) $8 + 8 + 8 + 8 + 8 + 8 = 48$

(2) $8 + 8 + 8 + 8 + 8 + 8 + 8 = 56$

(3) $8 + 8 + 8 + 8 + 8 + 8 + 8 + 8 = 64$

(4) $8 + 8 + 8 + 8 + 8 + 8 + 8 + 8 + 8 = 72$

(5) $8 + 8 + 8 + 8 + 8 + 8 + 8 + 8 + 8 + 8 = 80$

■ Write the numbers in the number line. Then add the numbers below.

| 48 | | | | |

(1) $8 + 8 + 8 + 8 + 8 + 8 =$

(2) $8 + 8 + 8 + 8 + 8 + 8 + 8 =$

(3) $8 + 8 + 8 + 8 + 8 + 8 + 8 + 8 =$

(4) $8 + 8 + 8 + 8 + 8 + 8 + 8 + 8 + 8 =$

(5) $8 + 8 + 8 + 8 + 8 + 8 + 8 + 8 + 8 + 8 =$

Multiplication 8

8×1 to 8×10

Name

Date

■ Read the multiplication table aloud.

Multiplication Table

(1)	8	×	1	= 8	Eight times one is eight.
(2)	8	×	2	= 16	Eight times two is sixteen.
(3)	8	×	3	= 24	Eight times three is twenty-four.
(4)	8	×	4	= 32	Eight times four is thirty-two.
(5)	8	×	5	= 40	Eight times five is forty.
(6)	8	×	6	= 48	Eight times six is forty-eight.
(7)	8	×	7	= 56	Eight times seven is fifty-six.
(8)	8	×	8	= 64	Eight times eight is sixty-four.
(9)	8	×	9	= 72	Eight times nine is seventy-two.
(10)	8	×	10	= 80	Eight times ten is eighty.

■ Read each number sentence aloud as you trace the answer.

(1) $8 \times 1 = 8$

(2) $8 \times 2 = 16$

(3) $8 \times 3 = 24$

(4) $8 \times 4 = 32$

(5) $8 \times 5 = 40$

(6) $8 \times 6 = 48$

(7) $8 \times 7 = 56$

(8) $8 \times 8 = 64$

(9) $8 \times 9 = 72$

(10) $8 \times 10 = 80$

■ Multiply the numbers below.

(1) $8 \times 1 =$

(2) $8 \times 2 =$

(3) $8 \times 3 =$

(4) $8 \times 4 =$

(5) $8 \times 5 =$

(6) $8 \times 6 =$

(7) $8 \times 7 =$

(8) $8 \times 8 =$

(9) $8 \times 9 =$

(10) $8 \times 10 =$

(11) $8 \times 1 =$

(12) $8 \times 2 =$

(13) $8 \times 3 =$

(14) $8 \times 4 =$

(15) $8 \times 5 =$

(16) $8 \times 6 =$

(17) $8 \times 7 =$

(18) $8 \times 8 =$

(19) $8 \times 9 =$

(20) $8 \times 10 =$

Name

Date

■ Multiply the numbers below.

(1) $8 \times 3 =$

(2) $8 \times 6 =$

(3) $8 \times 9 =$

(4) $8 \times 5 =$

(5) $8 \times 1 =$

(6) $8 \times 7 =$

(7) $8 \times 2 =$

(8) $8 \times 8 =$

(9) $8 \times 10 =$

(10) $8 \times 4 =$

(11) $8 \times 9 =$

(12) $8 \times 1 =$

(13) $8 \times 7 =$

(14) $8 \times 10 =$

(15) $8 \times 8 =$

(16) $8 \times 3 =$

(17) $8 \times 5 =$

(18) $8 \times 2 =$

(19) $8 \times 4 =$

(20) $8 \times 6 =$

■ Multiply the numbers below.

(1) 8 × 4 =

(2) 8 × 7 =

(3) 8 × 10 =

(4) 8 × 2 =

(5) 8 × 6 =

(6) 8 × 1 =

(7) 8 × 8 =

(8) 8 × 3 =

(9) 8 × 9 =

(10) 8 × 5 =

(11) 8 × 9 =

(12) 8 × 3 =

(13) 8 × 1 =

(14) 8 × 4 =

(15) 8 × 10 =

(16) 8 × 5 =

(17) 8 × 7 =

(18) 8 × 2 =

(19) 8 × 8 =

(20) 8 × 6 =

22 Multiplication 8
8×1 to 8×10

■ Multiply the numbers below.

(1) 8 × 7 =

(2) 8 × 3 =

(3) 8 × 6 =

(4) 8 × 1 =

(5) 8 × 10 =

(6) 8 × 5 =

(7) 8 × 9 =

(8) 8 × 4 =

(9) 8 × 2 =

(10) 8 × 8 =

(11) 8 × 2 =

(12) 8 × 5 =

(13) 8 × 9 =

(14) 8 × 7 =

(15) 8 × 3 =

(16) 8 × 1 =

(17) 8 × 8 =

(18) 8 × 6 =

(19) 8 × 4 =

(20) 8 × 10 =

■ Multiply the numbers below.

(1) $8 \times 1 =$

(2) $8 \times 8 =$

(3) $8 \times 10 =$

(4) $8 \times 3 =$

(5) $8 \times 6 =$

(6) $8 \times 2 =$

(7) $8 \times 7 =$

(8) $8 \times 4 =$

(9) $8 \times 5 =$

(10) $8 \times 9 =$

(11) $8 \times 4 =$

(12) $8 \times 9 =$

(13) $8 \times 1 =$

(14) $8 \times 5 =$

(15) $8 \times 10 =$

(16) $8 \times 6 =$

(17) $8 \times 2 =$

(18) $8 \times 8 =$

(19) $8 \times 3 =$

(20) $8 \times 7 =$

Name

Date

■ Multiply the numbers below.

(1) $6 \times 1 =$

(2) $6 \times 2 =$

(3) $6 \times 3 =$

(4) $7 \times 4 =$

(5) $7 \times 5 =$

(6) $7 \times 6 =$

(7) $8 \times 7 =$

(8) $8 \times 8 =$

(9) $8 \times 9 =$

(10) $8 \times 10 =$

(11) $6 \times 10 =$

(12) $7 \times 3 =$

(13) $8 \times 4 =$

(14) $6 \times 9 =$

(15) $7 \times 2 =$

(16) $8 \times 1 =$

(17) $6 \times 7 =$

(18) $7 \times 8 =$

(19) $8 \times 2 =$

(20) $8 \times 5 =$

Multiplication 6, 7, 8

■ Multiply the numbers below.

(1) $6 \times 9 =$

(2) $7 \times 7 =$

(3) $8 \times 5 =$

(4) $8 \times 6 =$

(5) $6 \times 1 =$

(6) $7 \times 8 =$

(7) $8 \times 10 =$

(8) $7 \times 3 =$

(9) $6 \times 2 =$

(10) $8 \times 4 =$

(11) $7 \times 10 =$

(12) $6 \times 3 =$

(13) $8 \times 1 =$

(14) $6 \times 8 =$

(15) $7 \times 5 =$

(16) $6 \times 6 =$

(17) $8 \times 2 =$

(18) $7 \times 4 =$

(19) $8 \times 9 =$

(20) $6 \times 7 =$

Practicing Numbers
1-90

Name

Date

■ Say each number aloud as you trace it.

1	2	3	4	5	6	7	8	9	10
11	12	13	14	15	16	17	18	19	20
21	22	23	24	25	26	27	28	29	30
31	32	33	34	35	36	37	38	39	40
41	42	43	44	45	46	47	48	49	50
51	52	53	54	55	56	57	58	59	60
61	62	63	64	65	66	67	68	69	70
71	72	73	74	75	76	77	78	79	80
81	82	83	84	85	86	87	88	89	90
91	92	93	94	95	96	97	98	99	100

9	18	27	36	45	54	63	72	81	90

■ Draw a line from 9 to 90 in order while saying each number aloud.

■ Add the numbers below.

(1) $9 + 9 = 18$

(2) $9 + 9 + 9 = 27$

(3) $9 + 9 + 9 + 9 = 36$

(4) $9 + 9 + 9 + 9 + 9 = 45$

(5) $9 + 9 + 9 + 9 + 9 + 9 = 54$

(6) $9 + 9 + 9 + 9 + 9 + 9 + 9 = 63$

(7) $9 + 9 + 9 + 9 + 9 + 9 + 9 + 9 = 72$

(8) $9 + 9 + 9 + 9 + 9 + 9 + 9 + 9 + 9 = 81$

(9) $9 + 9 + 9 + 9 + 9 + 9 + 9 + 9 + 9 + 9 = 90$

Name

Date

■ Say each number aloud as you trace it.

| 9 | 18 | 27 | 36 | 45 |

(1) $9 + 9 = 18$

(2) $9 + 9 + 9 = 27$

(3) $9 + 9 + 9 + 9 = 36$

(4) $9 + 9 + 9 + 9 + 9 = 45$

■ Write the numbers on the number line. Then add the numbers below.

| 9 | | | | |

(1) $9 + 9 =$

(2) $9 + 9 + 9 =$

(3) $9 + 9 + 9 + 9 =$

(4) $9 + 9 + 9 + 9 + 9 =$

■ Say each number aloud as you trace it.

54	63	72	81	90

(1) $9 + 9 + 9 + 9 + 9 + 9 = 54$

(2) $9 + 9 + 9 + 9 + 9 + 9 + 9 = 63$

(3) $9 + 9 + 9 + 9 + 9 + 9 + 9 + 9 = 72$

(4) $9 + 9 + 9 + 9 + 9 + 9 + 9 + 9 + 9 = 81$

(5) $9 + 9 + 9 + 9 + 9 + 9 + 9 + 9 + 9 + 9 = 90$

■ Write the numbers in the number line. Then add the numbers below.

54				

(1) $9 + 9 + 9 + 9 + 9 + 9 =$

(2) $9 + 9 + 9 + 9 + 9 + 9 + 9 =$

(3) $9 + 9 + 9 + 9 + 9 + 9 + 9 + 9 =$

(4) $9 + 9 + 9 + 9 + 9 + 9 + 9 + 9 + 9 =$

(5) $9 + 9 + 9 + 9 + 9 + 9 + 9 + 9 + 9 + 9 =$

Multiplication 9
9×1 to 9×10

Name

Date

■ Read the multiplication table aloud.

Multiplication Table

(1) $9 \times 1 = 9$ Nine times one is nine.

(2) $9 \times 2 = 18$ Nine times two is eighteen.

(3) $9 \times 3 = 27$ Nine times three is twenty-seven.

(4) $9 \times 4 = 36$ Nine times four is thirty-six.

(5) $9 \times 5 = 45$ Nine times five is forty-five.

(6) $9 \times 6 = 54$ Nine times six is fifty-four.

(7) $9 \times 7 = 63$ Nine times seven is sixty-three.

(8) $9 \times 8 = 72$ Nine times eight is seventy-two.

(9) $9 \times 9 = 81$ Nine times nine is eighty-one.

(10) $9 \times 10 = 90$ Nine times ten is ninety.

■ Read each number sentence aloud as you trace the answer.

(1) $9 \times 1 = 9$

(2) $9 \times 2 = 18$

(3) $9 \times 3 = 27$

(4) $9 \times 4 = 36$

(5) $9 \times 5 = 45$

(6) $9 \times 6 = 54$

(7) $9 \times 7 = 63$

(8) $9 \times 8 = 72$

(9) $9 \times 9 = 81$

(10) $9 \times 10 = 90$

9×1 to 9×10

■ Multiply the numbers below.

(1) 9 × 1 =

(2) 9 × 2 =

(3) 9 × 3 =

(4) 9 × 4 =

(5) 9 × 5 =

(6) 9 × 6 =

(7) 9 × 7 =

(8) 9 × 8 =

(9) 9 × 9 =

(10) 9 × 10 =

(11) 9 × 1 =

(12) 9 × 2 =

(13) 9 × 3 =

(14) 9 × 4 =

(15) 9 × 5 =

(16) 9 × 6 =

(17) 9 × 7 =

(18) 9 × 8 =

(19) 9 × 9 =

(20) 9 × 10 =

27 Multiplication 9
9×1 to 9×10

Name

Date

■ Multiply the numbers below.

(1) $9 \times 3 =$

(2) $9 \times 6 =$

(3) $9 \times 9 =$

(4) $9 \times 5 =$

(5) $9 \times 1 =$

(6) $9 \times 7 =$

(7) $9 \times 2 =$

(8) $9 \times 8 =$

(9) $9 \times 10 =$

(10) $9 \times 4 =$

(11) $9 \times 9 =$

(12) $9 \times 1 =$

(13) $9 \times 7 =$

(14) $9 \times 10 =$

(15) $9 \times 8 =$

(16) $9 \times 3 =$

(17) $9 \times 5 =$

(18) $9 \times 2 =$

(19) $9 \times 4 =$

(20) $9 \times 6 =$

■ Multiply the numbers below.

(1) $9 \times 7 =$

(2) $9 \times 4 =$

(3) $9 \times 10 =$

(4) $9 \times 2 =$

(5) $9 \times 6 =$

(6) $9 \times 1 =$

(7) $9 \times 8 =$

(8) $9 \times 3 =$

(9) $9 \times 9 =$

(10) $9 \times 5 =$

(11) $9 \times 9 =$

(12) $9 \times 3 =$

(13) $9 \times 1 =$

(14) $9 \times 4 =$

(15) $9 \times 10 =$

(16) $9 \times 5 =$

(17) $9 \times 7 =$

(18) $9 \times 2 =$

(19) $9 \times 8 =$

(20) $9 \times 6 =$

Name

Date

■ Multiply the numbers below.

(1) $9 \times 7 =$

(2) $9 \times 3 =$

(3) $9 \times 6 =$

(4) $9 \times 1 =$

(5) $9 \times 10 =$

(6) $9 \times 5 =$

(7) $9 \times 9 =$

(8) $9 \times 4 =$

(9) $9 \times 2 =$

(10) $9 \times 8 =$

(11) $9 \times 2 =$

(12) $9 \times 5 =$

(13) $9 \times 9 =$

(14) $9 \times 7 =$

(15) $9 \times 3 =$

(16) $9 \times 1 =$

(17) $9 \times 8 =$

(18) $9 \times 6 =$

(19) $9 \times 4 =$

(20) $9 \times 10 =$

■ Multiply the numbers below.

(1) $9 \times 1 =$

(2) $9 \times 8 =$

(3) $9 \times 10 =$

(4) $9 \times 3 =$

(5) $9 \times 6 =$

(6) $9 \times 2 =$

(7) $9 \times 7 =$

(8) $9 \times 4 =$

(9) $9 \times 5 =$

(10) $9 \times 9 =$

(11) $9 \times 4 =$

(12) $9 \times 9 =$

(13) $9 \times 1 =$

(14) $9 \times 5 =$

(15) $9 \times 10 =$

(16) $9 \times 6 =$

(17) $9 \times 2 =$

(18) $9 \times 8 =$

(19) $9 \times 3 =$

(20) $9 \times 7 =$

Name

Date

■ Multiply the numbers below.

(1) $7 \times 1 =$ (11) $7 \times 10 =$

(2) $7 \times 2 =$ (12) $8 \times 3 =$

(3) $7 \times 3 =$ (13) $9 \times 4 =$

(4) $8 \times 4 =$ (14) $7 \times 9 =$

(5) $8 \times 5 =$ (15) $8 \times 5 =$

(6) $8 \times 6 =$ (16) $9 \times 1 =$

(7) $9 \times 7 =$ (17) $7 \times 7 =$

(8) $9 \times 8 =$ (18) $8 \times 6 =$

(9) $9 \times 9 =$ (19) $9 \times 2 =$

(10) $9 \times 10 =$ (20) $9 \times 9 =$

Multiplication 7, 8, 9

■ Multiply the numbers below.

(1) $7 \times 9 =$

(2) $8 \times 7 =$

(3) $9 \times 5 =$

(4) $9 \times 6 =$

(5) $7 \times 1 =$

(6) $8 \times 8 =$

(7) $9 \times 10 =$

(8) $8 \times 3 =$

(9) $7 \times 2 =$

(10) $9 \times 4 =$

(11) $8 \times 10 =$

(12) $7 \times 3 =$

(13) $9 \times 1 =$

(14) $7 \times 8 =$

(15) $8 \times 5 =$

(16) $7 \times 6 =$

(17) $9 \times 2 =$

(18) $8 \times 4 =$

(19) $9 \times 9 =$

(20) $7 \times 7 =$

Name

Date

■ Say each number aloud as you trace it.

1	2	3	4	5	6	7	8	9	10
11	12	13	14	15	16	17	18	19	20
21	22	23	24	25	26	27	28	29	30
31	32	33	34	35	36	37	38	39	40
41	42	43	44	45	46	47	48	49	50
51	52	53	54	55	56	57	58	59	60
61	62	63	64	65	66	67	68	69	70
71	72	73	74	75	76	77	78	79	80
81	82	83	84	85	86	87	88	89	90
91	92	93	94	95	96	97	98	99	100

10	20	30	40	50	60	70	80	90	100

■ Draw a line from 10 to 100 in order while saying each number aloud.

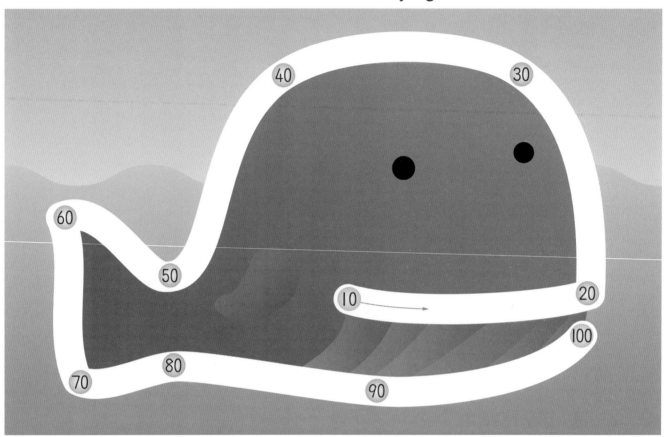

■ Add the numbers below.

(1) $10 + 10 = 20$

(2) $10 + 10 + 10 = 30$

(3) $10 + 10 + 10 + 10 = 40$

(4) $10 + 10 + 10 + 10 + 10 = 50$

(5) $10 + 10 + 10 + 10 + 10 + 10 = 60$

(6) $10 + 10 + 10 + 10 + 10 + 10 + 10 = 70$

(7) $10 + 10 + 10 + 10 + 10 + 10 + 10 + 10 = 80$

(8) $10 + 10 + 10 + 10 + 10 + 10 + 10 + 10 + 10 = 90$

(9) $10 + 10 + 10 + 10 + 10 + 10 + 10 + 10 + 10 + 10 = 100$

31 Practicing Repeated Addition

10–50

Name

Date

■ Say each number aloud as you trace it.

| 10 | 20 | 30 | 40 | 50 |

(1) 10 + 10 = 20

(2) 10 + 10 + 10 = 30

(3) 10 + 10 + 10 + 10 = 40

(4) 10 + 10 + 10 + 10 + 10 = 50

■ Write the numbers on the number line. Then add the numbers below.

| 10 | | | | |

(1) 10 + 10 =

(2) 10 + 10 + 10 =

(3) 10 + 10 + 10 + 10 =

(4) 10 + 10 + 10 + 10 + 10 =

■ Say each number aloud as you trace it.

60	70	80	90	100

(1) $10+10+10+10+10+10 = 60$

(2) $10+10+10+10+10+10+10 = 70$

(3) $10+10+10+10+10+10+10+10 = 80$

(4) $10+10+10+10+10+10+10+10+10 = 90$

(5) $10+10+10+10+10+10+10+10+10+10 = 100$

■ Write the numbers in the number line. Then add the numbers below.

60				

(1) $10+10+10+10+10+10 =$

(2) $10+10+10+10+10+10+10 =$

(3) $10+10+10+10+10+10+10+10 =$

(4) $10+10+10+10+10+10+10+10+10 =$

(5) $10+10+10+10+10+10+10+10+10+10 =$

Multiplication 10

10 × 1 to 10 × 10

Name

Date

■ Read the multiplication table aloud.

Multiplication Table

(1)	10 ×	1	=	10	Ten times one is ten.
(2)	10 ×	2	=	20	Ten times two is twenty.
(3)	10 ×	3	=	30	Ten times three is thirty.
(4)	10 ×	4	=	40	Ten times four is forty.
(5)	10 ×	5	=	50	Ten times five is fifty.
(6)	10 ×	6	=	60	Ten times six is sixty.
(7)	10 ×	7	=	70	Ten times seven is seventy.
(8)	10 ×	8	=	80	Ten times eight is eighty.
(9)	10 ×	9	=	90	Ten times nine is ninety.
(10)	10 ×	10	=	100	Ten times ten is one hundred.

■ Read each number sentence aloud as you trace the answer.

(1) $10 \times 1 = 10$

(2) $10 \times 2 = 20$

(3) $10 \times 3 = 30$

(4) $10 \times 4 = 40$

(5) $10 \times 5 = 50$

(6) $10 \times 6 = 60$

(7) $10 \times 7 = 70$

(8) $10 \times 8 = 80$

(9) $10 \times 9 = 90$

(10) $10 \times 10 = 100$

10×1 to 10×10

■ Multiply the numbers below.

(1) $10 \times 1 =$

(2) $10 \times 2 =$

(3) $10 \times 3 =$

(4) $10 \times 4 =$

(5) $10 \times 5 =$

(6) $10 \times 6 =$

(7) $10 \times 7 =$

(8) $10 \times 8 =$

(9) $10 \times 9 =$

(10) $10 \times 10 =$

(11) $10 \times 1 =$

(12) $10 \times 2 =$

(13) $10 \times 3 =$

(14) $10 \times 4 =$

(15) $10 \times 5 =$

(16) $10 \times 6 =$

(17) $10 \times 7 =$

(18) $10 \times 8 =$

(19) $10 \times 9 =$

(20) $10 \times 10 =$

33 Multiplication 10

10×1 to 10×10

■ Multiply the numbers below.

(1) $10 \times 3 =$

(2) $10 \times 6 =$

(3) $10 \times 9 =$

(4) $10 \times 5 =$

(5) $10 \times 1 =$

(6) $10 \times 7 =$

(7) $10 \times 2 =$

(8) $10 \times 8 =$

(9) $10 \times 10 =$

(10) $10 \times 4 =$

(11) $10 \times 9 =$

(12) $10 \times 1 =$

(13) $10 \times 7 =$

(14) $10 \times 10 =$

(15) $10 \times 8 =$

(16) $10 \times 3 =$

(17) $10 \times 5 =$

(18) $10 \times 2 =$

(19) $10 \times 4 =$

(20) $10 \times 6 =$

■ Multiply the numbers below.

(1) 10 × 4 =

(2) 10 × 7 =

(3) 10 × 10 =

(4) 10 × 2 =

(5) 10 × 6 =

(6) 10 × 1 =

(7) 10 × 8 =

(8) 10 × 3 =

(9) 10 × 9 =

(10) 10 × 5 =

(11) 10 × 9 =

(12) 10 × 3 =

(13) 10 × 1 =

(14) 10 × 4 =

(15) 10 × 10 =

(16) 10 × 5 =

(17) 10 × 7 =

(18) 10 × 2 =

(19) 10 × 8 =

(20) 10 × 6 =

Multiplication 10

10×1 to 10×10

Name

Date

■ Multiply the numbers below.

(1) $10 \times 7 =$

(2) $10 \times 3 =$

(3) $10 \times 6 =$

(4) $10 \times 1 =$

(5) $10 \times 10 =$

(6) $10 \times 5 =$

(7) $10 \times 9 =$

(8) $10 \times 4 =$

(9) $10 \times 2 =$

(10) $10 \times 8 =$

(11) $10 \times 2 =$

(12) $10 \times 5 =$

(13) $10 \times 9 =$

(14) $10 \times 7 =$

(15) $10 \times 3 =$

(16) $10 \times 1 =$

(17) $10 \times 8 =$

(18) $10 \times 6 =$

(19) $10 \times 4 =$

(20) $10 \times 10 =$

10×1 to 10×10

■ Multiply the numbers below.

(1) $10 \times 1 =$

(2) $10 \times 8 =$

(3) $10 \times 10 =$

(4) $10 \times 3 =$

(5) $10 \times 6 =$

(6) $10 \times 2 =$

(7) $10 \times 7 =$

(8) $10 \times 4 =$

(9) $10 \times 5 =$

(10) $10 \times 9 =$

(11) $10 \times 4 =$

(12) $10 \times 9 =$

(13) $10 \times 1 =$

(14) $10 \times 5 =$

(15) $10 \times 10 =$

(16) $10 \times 6 =$

(17) $10 \times 2 =$

(18) $10 \times 8 =$

(19) $10 \times 3 =$

(20) $10 \times 7 =$

Name

Date

■ Multiply the numbers below.

(1) $8 \times 1 =$

(2) $8 \times 2 =$

(3) $8 \times 3 =$

(4) $9 \times 4 =$

(5) $9 \times 5 =$

(6) $9 \times 6 =$

(7) $10 \times 7 =$

(8) $10 \times 8 =$

(9) $10 \times 9 =$

(10) $10 \times 10 =$

(11) $8 \times 10 =$

(12) $9 \times 3 =$

(13) $10 \times 4 =$

(14) $8 \times 9 =$

(15) $9 \times 2 =$

(16) $10 \times 1 =$

(17) $8 \times 7 =$

(18) $9 \times 9 =$

(19) $10 \times 2 =$

(20) $10 \times 6 =$

Multiplication 8, 9, 10

■ Multiply the numbers below.

(1) $8 \times 9 =$ (11) $9 \times 10 =$

(2) $9 \times 7 =$ (12) $8 \times 3 =$

(3) $10 \times 5 =$ (13) $10 \times 1 =$

(4) $10 \times 6 =$ (14) $8 \times 8 =$

(5) $8 \times 1 =$ (15) $9 \times 5 =$

(6) $9 \times 8 =$ (16) $9 \times 6 =$

(7) $9 \times 9 =$ (17) $10 \times 2 =$

(8) $10 \times 3 =$ (18) $9 \times 4 =$

(9) $8 \times 2 =$ (19) $10 \times 9 =$

(10) $10 \times 4 =$ (20) $8 \times 7 =$

36 Review
Multiplication 6 – 10

Name

Date

■ Multiply the numbers below.

(1) $6 \times 3 =$

(2) $7 \times 7 =$

(3) $8 \times 9 =$

(4) $9 \times 4 =$

(5) $10 \times 6 =$

(6) $9 \times 8 =$

(7) $6 \times 5 =$

(8) $7 \times 10 =$

(9) $10 \times 2 =$

(10) $8 \times 8 =$

(11) $9 \times 2 =$

(12) $8 \times 3 =$

(13) $10 \times 9 =$

(14) $6 \times 10 =$

(15) $7 \times 5 =$

(16) $9 \times 9 =$

(17) $10 \times 4 =$

(18) $6 \times 7 =$

(19) $7 \times 8 =$

(20) $8 \times 1 =$

Multiplication 6 −10

■ Multiply the numbers below.

(1) $10 \times 1 =$

(2) $6 \times 2 =$

(3) $7 \times 4 =$

(4) $8 \times 6 =$

(5) $9 \times 10 =$

(6) $6 \times 6 =$

(7) $7 \times 8 =$

(8) $8 \times 7 =$

(9) $9 \times 3 =$

(10) $10 \times 4 =$

(11) $7 \times 10 =$

(12) $8 \times 2 -$

(13) $9 \times 1 =$

(14) $10 \times 8 =$

(15) $6 \times 5 =$

(16) $8 \times 4 =$

(17) $9 \times 2 =$

(18) $10 \times 3 =$

(19) $6 \times 9 =$

(20) $7 \times 7 =$

■ Multiply the numbers below.

(1) $9 \times 2 =$

(2) $6 \times 7 =$

(3) $8 \times 9 =$

(4) $10 \times 4 =$

(5) $7 \times 6 =$

(6) $8 \times 10 =$

(7) $6 \times 1 =$

(8) $9 \times 7 =$

(9) $7 \times 2 =$

(10) $10 \times 5 =$

(11) $10 \times 2 =$

(12) $7 \times 3 =$

(13) $9 \times 9 =$

(14) $6 \times 10 =$

(15) $8 \times 5 =$

(16) $7 \times 9 =$

(17) $6 \times 4 =$

(18) $10 \times 7 =$

(19) $7 \times 8 =$

(20) $8 \times 1 =$

Multiplication 6 – 10

■ Multiply the numbers below.

(1) $6 \times 4 =$

(2) $8 \times 2 =$

(3) $10 \times 9 =$

(4) $7 \times 6 =$

(5) $9 \times 10 =$

(6) $7 \times 1 =$

(7) $10 \times 8 =$

(8) $8 \times 7 =$

(9) $6 \times 3 =$

(10) $9 \times 5 =$

(11) $10 \times 10 =$

(12) $8 \times 3 =$

(13) $9 \times 1 =$

(14) $6 \times 8 =$

(15) $7 \times 5 =$

(16) $8 \times 6 =$

(17) $6 \times 2 =$

(18) $9 \times 4 =$

(19) $7 \times 9 =$

(20) $10 \times 7 =$

38 Review
Multiplication 1-10

Name

Date

■ Multiply the numbers below.

(1) $1 \times 5 =$

(2) $1 \times 10 =$

(3) $2 \times 4 =$

(4) $2 \times 8 =$

(5) $3 \times 6 =$

(6) $3 \times 2 =$

(7) $4 \times 9 =$

(8) $4 \times 1 =$

(9) $5 \times 3 =$

(10) $5 \times 7 =$

(11) $6 \times 3 =$

(12) $6 \times 9 =$

(13) $7 \times 2 =$

(14) $7 \times 4 =$

(15) $8 \times 1 =$

(16) $8 \times 8 =$

(17) $9 \times 5 =$

(18) $9 \times 7 =$

(19) $10 \times 6 =$

(20) $10 \times 10 =$

Multiplication 1–10

■ Multiply the numbers below.

(1) $1 \times 3 =$

(2) $2 \times 5 =$

(3) $3 \times 8 =$

(4) $4 \times 10 =$

(5) $5 \times 6 =$

(6) $6 \times 1 =$

(7) $7 \times 7 =$

(8) $8 \times 4 =$

(9) $9 \times 2 =$

(10) $10 \times 9 =$

(11) $1 \times 9 =$

(12) $2 \times 6 =$

(13) $3 \times 4 =$

(14) $4 \times 5 =$

(15) $5 \times 8 =$

(16) $6 \times 7 =$

(17) $7 \times 1 =$

(18) $8 \times 10 =$

(19) $9 \times 3 =$

(20) $10 \times 2 =$

Name

Date

■ Multiply the numbers below.

(1) $4 \times 3 =$

(2) $8 \times 2 =$

(3) $7 \times 1 =$

(4) $10 \times 8 =$

(5) $5 \times 9 =$

(6) $6 \times 7 =$

(7) $1 \times 4 =$

(8) $2 \times 6 =$

(9) $3 \times 5 =$

(10) $9 \times 10 =$

(11) $2 \times 7 =$

(12) $6 \times 1 =$

(13) $3 \times 9 =$

(14) $4 \times 5 =$

(15) $10 \times 2 =$

(16) $1 \times 8 =$

(17) $9 \times 4 =$

(18) $5 \times 6 =$

(19) $7 \times 10 =$

(20) $8 \times 3 =$

Multiplication 1-10

■ Multiply the numbers below.

(1) $9 \times 3 =$

(2) $8 \times 5 =$

(3) $5 \times 8 =$

(4) $3 \times 10 =$

(5) $2 \times 6 =$

(6) $1 \times 1 =$

(7) $4 \times 7 =$

(8) $10 \times 4 =$

(9) $6 \times 2 =$

(10) $7 \times 9 =$

(11) $1 \times 2 =$

(12) $10 \times 3 =$

(13) $7 \times 8 =$

(14) $4 \times 9 =$

(15) $8 \times 6 =$

(16) $5 \times 1 =$

(17) $3 \times 7 =$

(18) $2 \times 10 =$

(19) $9 \times 4 =$

(20) $6 \times 5 =$

Name

Date

■ Multiply the numbers below.

(1) $7 \times 9 =$

(2) $6 \times 5 =$

(3) $4 \times 8 =$

(4) $2 \times 7 =$

(5) $7 \times 8 =$

(6) $5 \times 1 =$

(7) $9 \times 4 =$

(8) $3 \times 9 =$

(9) $5 \times 4 =$

(10) $2 \times 2 =$

(11) $1 \times 7 =$

(12) $9 \times 3 =$

(13) $7 \times 6 =$

(14) $4 \times 5 =$

(15) $9 \times 9 =$

(16) $2 \times 6 =$

(17) $10 \times 9 =$

(18) $5 \times 6 =$

(19) $8 \times 5 =$

(20) $6 \times 8 =$

Multiplication 1−10

To parents
Multiplication is a difficult skill to master. Make sure to congratulate your child for completing this workbook! If your child needs a little more practice, try *Grade 3 Multiplication* from our Kumon Math Workbooks series.

■ Multiply the numbers below.

(1) $7 \times 3 =$

(2) $8 \times 4 =$

(3) $9 \times 8 =$

(4) $5 \times 8 =$

(5) $10 \times 7 =$

(6) $2 \times 4 =$

(7) $3 \times 9 =$

(8) $6 \times 8 =$

(9) $7 \times 7 =$

(10) $4 \times 3 =$

(11) $9 \times 6 =$

(12) $7 \times 9 =$

(13) $8 \times 8 =$

(14) $5 \times 4 =$

(15) $6 \times 6 =$

(16) $7 \times 2 =$

(17) $4 \times 9 =$

(18) $9 \times 9 =$

(19) $3 \times 8 =$

(20) $10 \times 10 =$

Certificate of Achievement

is hereby congratulated on completing

My Book of Multiplication

Presented on _____ , 20___

_____
Parent or Guardian

$7 \times 8 = 56$